BLUFF YOUR WAY IN ARCHAEOLOGY

PAUL BAHN

RAVETTE BOOKS

Published by Ravette Books Limited
3 Glenside Estate, Star Road
Partridge Green, Horsham
West Sussex RH13 8RA
(0403) 710392

First printed 1989
Reprinted 1991

Series Editor – Anne Tauté

Cover design – Jim Wire
Typesetting – Input Typesetting Ltd.
Printing & binding – Cox & Wyman Ltd.
Production – Oval Projects Ltd.

The Bluffer's Guides are based on
an original idea by Peter Wolfe.

CONTENTS

THE AUTHOR

Dating from 1953, Paul Bahn decided at an early age that he wanted to be an archaeologist since it seemed to be better than working for a living. As a child he dug holes in his back garden in Hull and found fragments of pottery, which proved to be Willow Pattern (Woolworths) and not Ancient Roman, but the thrill of discovery remained intact.

He later studied archaeology at Cambridge, obtained his Ph.D., and adopted the regulation beard and shapeless sweaters, but despite weeks of cutting through the South American jungle in search of lost settlements, he failed to acquire a taste for either tobacco or vast quantities of alcohol.

He therefore settled for freelance writing about what he considers to be the more interesting aspects of the subject such as horse teeth and engravings of genitalia (viz: *Crib Biting: Tethered Horses in the Palaeolithic?*; *No Sex, Please, We're Aurignacians*).

Paul Bahn's latest books are the brick-like text on *Archaeology* co-authored with Colin Renfrew, and *Easter Island, Earth Island* co-authored with John Flenley. His lavishly illustrated *Images of the Ice Age* is highly spoken of in certain obscure circles: the public liked it too.

Fortunately all this work entails a certain amount of travel which is why this book was written on a beach in Fiji rather than in a portakabin by a rained-off rescue dig in Milton Keynes.

INTRODUCTION

What is Archaeology?

If History is bunk, then Archaeology is junk. This bizarre subject entails seeking, retrieving and studying the abandoned, lost, broken and discarded traces left by human beings in the past. Archaeologists are therefore the precise opposite of dustmen, though they often dress like them.

Little did ancient peoples* suspect that the garbage they so readily discarded would one day be resurrected by these scientific rag-and-bone merchants. Had they suspected, they might have taken better care of things, and attached some handy labels to explain the objects and what they did with them. As they didn't, archaeologists have to try to figure it all out for themselves.

Archaeology is rather like a vast, fiendish jigsaw puzzle invented by the devil as an instrument of tantalising torment, since:

a) it will never be finished
b) you don't know how many pieces are missing
c) most of them are lost for ever
d) you can't cheat by looking at the picture.

Prehistoric persons did not always have the foresight to use materials like stone or pottery that survive the ages, and untold quantities of objects have decayed and disappeared. This is bad news for the archaeologist, but wonderful news for you.

There are several reasons why Archaeology is an

---

* A seasoned bluffer can gain an important advantage early in any conversation by pouncing fiercely on any use of terms such as 'man, mankind, manmade, early man, fossil man, Neanderthal Man, man the hunter', and so forth, as being naively and offensively sexist. This should put your opponent off balance for some time.

ideal subject in which to become an accomplished bluffer:

1. Much of the time, the evidence is so patchy that anyone's guess is as valid as anyone else's. You can't prove anything. Where the remote past is concerned, nobody *knows* what took place. The best that can be offered is an informed guess. This you should dress up with the grand title of 'deduction' or 'theory', or (grander still) 'hypothesis'.

2. It is particularly easy to bluff your way through a conversation about archaeology with a non-archaeologist. This is due to the fact that though most people profess an interest in the past, their eyes tend to glaze over after a few minutes on the subject.

3. It is especially easy in this field to pass yourself off as an expert, full of impressive and esoteric knowledge, because it is filled with obscure terms and exotic names and places. Even if the general public has heard of them, it is almost certain they will know little or nothing about them. Thus a minimum of homework will go a very long way.

It is therefore child's play to give the false impression of being informed, and few will dare to challenge your facts or your hypotheses.

Any inkling that your audience forms part of the huge number of people who, thanks to movies and cartoons, believe that early humans lived alongside dinosaurs, can similarly be used as an opportunity for a derisive snort or a pitying sigh before you enlighten them about the gap of many millions of years between the two lifeforms.

Never let the fact that nothing is really known about past events stand in your way: instead, use it to your advantage. Some eminent archaeologists have built their entire careers upon convincing bluff.

BEING AN ARCHAEOLOGIST

It takes very special qualities to devote one's life to problems with no attainable solutions and to poking around in dead people's garbage: words like 'masochistic', 'nosy' and 'completely batty' spring readily to mind. This is why eccentricity is a hallmark of the profession. So is an addiction to alcohol (in fact archaeology could be a synonym for alcoholism). You can wryly attribute this fact either to the need to drown one's sorrows in the face of unattainable solutions, or simply to acute embarrassment at practising an inherently ridiculous and often futile profession.

The popular image of archaeologists is that of a bunch of absent-minded scruffs and misfits covered in dust and cobwebs. The bluffer will stress, however, with a knowing smile, that this is not always true – some of them are only slightly absent-minded, and a few keep quite clean.

You can recognise an archetypal archaeologist from the beard, curved pipe, shapeless sweater or T-shirt, and sandals or hiking boots – and that's only the women. The pipe is usually an affectation, designed to convey the false impression that the archaeologist is a real Sherlock Holmes – a classic prop in bluffing. Beards lend an air of wisdom and maturity, but are basically a means of getting an extra five minutes in bed. The sweaters serve to conceal innumerable figure flaws (most commonly caused by too much beer) while T-shirts unfortunately draw attention to them.

Clothing and footwear depend on temperature, conditions and income, and are often worn for days or weeks without being changed. It is important to pretend to believe that this is caused by remoteness from a water-source or laundrette, and is not attributable to a low standard of personal hygiene, or simply sheer lack of interest.

Most archaeologists, if asked why they devote their lives to the subject, will wax lyrical about:
- their passion for the past
- their desire to make a modest contribution to piecing together our picture of human development and history.

Some will even claim that, like Schliemann, they have pursued this goal singlemindedly since childhood.

Don't believe a word of it: as a good bluffer you should be able to recognize self-serving twaddle at twenty paces. If a group of archaeologists were transported into the past in a time machine, the chances are that they would be thoroughly stupefied within a few hours, and yearning for air conditioning, real ale, and their own version of how things might have been in the past.

In reality most people are attracted to archaeology for a variety of more practical reasons. Here are the main five.

1. To have fun. This is, on occasions, quite possible: it has even been described as the most fun you can have with your pants on.

2. To have an activity/adventure holiday and meet people of the opposite sex. If you get jaded spending your spare time lying on a beach and reading a thriller, and want to get away from package-tourists, then some archaeological fieldwork may seem like the ideal solution. Most field directors insist that you join up for at least a fortnight. This is so that you can't flee in horror when you discover that you are just unpaid labour and trapped in a group of equally tiresome people, many of whom take the work extremely seriously.

3. To follow a university course that is generally regarded as cushier than most. At the end of it, some students decide to go on to do a Ph.D., either because they can think of nothing better to do, or because they can't face entering the real world and finding a proper job. As it is, many drop out along the way. Of those that get their Ph.D., most find there are no jobs in archaeology, they have wasted several years, and that all that remains is to retrain as an accountant or tax inspector. Here their passion for the past quickly withers, to be replaced by mammon and middle age.

4. To make a living (not recommended unless your material needs are minimal). As Champollion said, archaeology is a beautiful mistress but she brings a poor dowry.

5. To make a career. This is not easy, for an archaeologist's career lies in ruins from the start.

An archaeological career is considered successful if the archaeologist becomes:
- a national celebrity (rare)
- an international celebrity (very rare)
- or wealthy (extremely rare – 'wealth' and 'archaeological career' are almost contradictions in terms).

This is usually done by making an important discovery with public appeal. Virtually all professional archaeologists today stress that they are not treasure-hunters but scientists, seeking information rather than objects. Therefore, in any conversation that focuses on individual treasures, the bluffer can score points by emphasising, with great condescension, that nowadays archaeologists dig not to find things but to find *out* things.

This is generally true, but it is also fair to say that

9

any archaeologist would be overjoyed to find something that not only proved important to the subject but which also caught the public imagination. And since very few discoveries, if presented soberly, would rouse more than a stifled yawn from the average television viewer or tabloid reader, they have to be dressed up with bluffers' superlatives: the first, the oldest, the biggest, the best-preserved, richest, most spectacular of their kind.

Another effective ploy is to associate the find with a perennially popular topic such as:
- sex
- gore
- cannibalism.

Remember, too, that since the public cares little for anonymous ancestors, it is crucial to link the find to a well-known historical or legendary figure, preferably royal (King Arthur is a firm favourite). The discovery of the umpteenth Roman skeleton or Peruvian pot will arouse no interest, but if you present them as possibly Julius Caesar's grandmother or Atahualpa's spitoon, you will hit the headlines and perhaps even the chat-shows. Your colleagues may sneer but will be green with envy when they see the exposure and increased funding that this sort of thing will get you.

As a bluffer, you should pour scorn on all such attention seeking as 'tubthumping by unscrupulous and ambitious careerists'. If accused of it yourself you should explain that, sadly, this kind of thing is a necessary evil to keep archaeology in the public eye, and that you allowed your work to be distorted by the media only with the greatest reluctance and with no thought of furthering your career.

It will come as no surprise therefore to discover that anyone who takes up archaeology as a profession is, or has to become, a consummate bluffer.

Students are novice bluffers, trying to learn the rudiments of the subject in order to bluff their way through examinations and into a career or, at least, a degree. This entails a certain amount of reading and writing, but also some participation in mundane fieldwork in order to gain experience and ingratiate themselves with their teachers.

Lecturers usually have a large teaching workload and cannot therefore be expected to think and be original as well. They are practised bluffers through having to convince their audience that they know lots of things outside their particular field of interest, and have not swotted it all up the night before. Unlike lecturers in most other subjects, their real work starts in the summer vacation when they may do a bit of research, or direct some fieldwork, or try to make some headway with the book they've been meaning to write for years. Their main goal is to get a better salary and a reduced workload by becoming

Senior Academics, i.e. advanced bluffers. Once these dizzy heights have been reached, it is possible to sit back and rest on your laurels: for example, one archaeological head-of-department in northern England has done absolutely nothing since the appearance of a thesis 20 years ago, and is therefore nicknamed 'Thrombosis', the clot that blocks up the system. Others tread water by constantly producing variations on the same piece of work. One or two manage to remain fresh and inventive, and produce interesting work, but they are exceptions and out of place in a book on bluffing.

Note that none of these more advanced positions will give an ounce of glory to the **Secretaries** who are the most important people in academic archaeology, as

11

they are usually the sanest individuals in the subject, they do all the hard work, and without them most academics and departments would simply fall apart.

Professional archaeologists need to take a vow of poverty, though not, fortunately, one of chastity. Most of them choose to substitute interest or leisure for income. Being slender of means (though broad of belly), they constantly have to apply and beg for grants:

a)   to do fieldwork
b)   to attend conferences
c)   to get things published.

You should know that these applications never tell the truth about the low degree of importance or originality in the project, but rather stress the potentially crucial and fascinating nature of the work.

It is sad but true to say that:

●   The only way to make good money from archaeology is to bluff your way to becoming a Professor.

●   The only way to make excellent money is to sport tight jeans and designer stubble (on chin and chest), get on television, talk with breathless enthusiasm, and bluff the public into thinking you are an expert on the subject.

●   The only way to make vast amounts of money from it is to write *The Clan of the Cave Bear*.

TYPES OF ARCHAEOLOGIST

There are two basic categories: the Field Archaeologist and the Armchair Archaeologist.

Field Archaeologists are often called 'Dirt Archaeologists', a term that may not necessarily apply to their minds or their appearance, though it often does. They are the ones who actually go out and dig or survey in order to obtain some evidence to investigate. They are also the ones who try to live up to their new 'Action Man' image as swashbuckling bullwhip-wielders, usually with a marked lack of success.

Field Archaeologists can generally bluff an audience into believing their work is exciting and full of thrills; but you should know that, just like the world of moviemaking or fashion photography, while it may look glamorous and enviable from the outside, if you try it you soon discover the long periods of nothing much happening.

There are compensations, of course: few other occupations enable you to go off into the wilds at regular intervals with a bunch of nubile youngsters who are eager to have fun and obtain good grades. This is why many long-suffering non-archaeological spouses feel obliged to go along too.

Field Archaeologists tend to get sunburn, insect bites, blistered hands/knees/feet, the runs, and frequent hangovers.

Armchair Archaeologists choose their role for a variety of reasons: laziness, incompetence, an unwillingness to dirty their hands, or an aversion to sunlight.

They sustain the traditional image of archaeologists as dreary old fogies or, in many cases, young fogies. As they cannot or will not obtain evidence of their own, they have to turn to other people's. Nevertheless they can achieve real eminence in the subject by practising a special kind of bluffing known as 'Theoretical Archaeology'. This is done in several ways:

1. You conceal your lack of data by questioning the validity of everyone else's:
    – How well was the site dug?
    – How representative was the sample?

2. You deflect attention from your own lack of ideas and solutions by attacking those trying to do some work and by trying to demolish their whole approach to the subject.

This bullying and sermonising has paid amazing dividends in many careers, particularly within the 'New Archeology'. If you are sufficiently loud, rude and aggressive, generations of students will come to treat you with extraordinary respect and deference. This is known as the 'Alpha Baboon Syndrome', since monkeys achieve dominance with the same kind of blustering bluff.

But behaviour alone is not sufficient: you will actually need to say or print something. Theoretical archaeologists (or 'the Living Dead', as they are known) put out enormous quantities of papers and books, filled with:
a) impressive jargon
b) long words
c) mathematical equations
d) complicated diagrams involving a mass of lines, arrows and boxes.

Few people ever read this stuff apart from other theoreticians trying to keep up with new jargon (and looking for something new to attack), and those students unfortunate enough to have the authors among their teachers.

Consequently, very few people ever realize that much of the text is meaningless, the equations pointless, and the diagrams superfluous, so the industry keeps on rolling along. Here is a genuine example of a sentence from a theoretical work:

'The notion of structural contradictions resulting in societal change relates to the operation of causative variables at a different epistemological level from that assumed in analysis of interlinked variables and entities resulting in morphogenic feedback processes.'

Despite its apparent sophistication, this kind of bluffing is remarkably easy: just learn a few key words like cognitive, interpretive (*not* interpretative – this is primarily an American skill) and operationalize (ditto); then string them together with appropriate jargon like structuralist, processual or even post-processual (don't worry about what all this means – nobody else knows or cares either), and you can waffle happily until your audience/readers doze off or flee in terror.

If you are ever confronted by a frightening number of theoretical archaeologists (two), you should first try to talk positively about the merits of fieldwork. If they persist, try quoting Kant's dictum that 'concepts without percepts are empty' (i.e. you can't get a grasp of the whole without delving into some minutiae – in other words, get on and do some real work). Criticism by a real German philosopher should strike to their very heart, or at least stun them long enough for you to make your excuses and your escape.

Armchair Archaeologists tend to get ulcers, egomania, and permanent hangovers.

The difference can be summed up very simply: Field Archaeologists dig up rubbish, Theoretical Archaeologists write it down.

ARCHAEOLOGY IN THE FIELD

At some point in their careers, most archaeologists, with the exception of theoreticians, actually go outside and try to obtain some fresh information.

Finding Sites

The simplest way to find sites is to ask somebody who knows where they are. The smart bluffer should be aware that the most important sites are not found by archaeologists at all – instead they are found accidentally by farmers, quarrymen, construction workers, or aerial photographers; underwater sites are discovered by fishermen and divers; caves have been found by potholers, children (in the case of Lascaux), even dogs (in the case of Altamira); and professional tomb-robbers (say "huaqueros" for Latin America, "tombaroli" for Italy) are far more adept at finding ancient graves than any archaeologists. However, it is the latter who investigate the sites and who get all the publicity and the kudos.

The particular area where they choose to work is supposedly selected in order to answer questions of specific relevance to their research interest. In practice the real reasons involve some or all of the following factors:

- the climate
- the presence of a lover
- swimming facilities
- the local booze.

For these reasons France is particularly popular. It

also offers superb food and a sensible French tendency to put roofs over their excavations.

Another important factor is the political situation – warfare is not a healthy background for archaeological fieldwork. This is why most American archaeologists left Iran when the Ayatollah came to power. Unfortunately, some chose to move to the short-lived safety of Afghanistan.

Whatever the area, there are two principal ways to get new information: excavation and survey.

Excavation

The public thinks that archaeologists spend all their time digging. In fact, not all of them dig, and only a few dig all the time. The bluffer should explain condescendingly that processing and analysing the finds usually takes far longer than the excavation itself, which is therefore just the foreplay, the preliminary stage: the means to an end, not an end in itself.

Any excavation that the public can reach is likely to be visited with annoying frequency by honest citizens who think it is there for their amusement. They should be treated with the greatest courtesy and respect in case:

a) they may wish to contribute financially to the project,

or b) they are connected to someone important who might be able to shut down the work.

Depending on their opinion of the visitors, directors may assign the most charming or the most obnoxious digger to the task of giving guided tours. Directors will usually take on this chore themselves only for VIPs.

Visitors generally offer a limited range of questions

and comments, and bluffers should familiarise themselves with the most irritating in order to prepare
witty responses worthy of G. B. Shaw or Oscar Wilde:

- Found any gold, then?
- Keep going, you might reach Australia, harhar.
- How old is that? How do you know?
- Why did people live in holes in the ground?
- Lost a contact lens, have you?
- Is that a dinosaur bone?
- Would you like to come and dig my garden when
  you've finished?
- Where's your hat and whip, Indiana?
- What do you do when it rains?
- I think Michael Wood's really terrific, don't you?

It has been said that there is no standard or correct
way to dig a site, but plenty of wrong ways. This is a
useful tip for the bluffer in charge of such a project.
You can dismiss any criticism of method as being inap-
plicable to the particular and unique circumstances
present at the site.

In fact, there are two basic ways to dig:

vertically (to see the different layers), and
horizontally (to expose wider areas of a particular
layer).

Most directors keep their strategies flexible to take
advantage of any special features they may encounter,
or to camouflage any mistakes that may be made. So
you should know that rather than being carefully
planned from the start, most digs muddle along by
trowel and error.

It is advisable, however, to get as much information
as you can about what lies beneath the surface before
you start digging. This helps to avoid the embarrassment of:

a) finding you're digging in the wrong place
b) not finding anything
c) finding far more than you were prepared for.

So a whole range of sophisticated techniques and gadgets can be unleashed, which allow boffins or the more technically minded students to produce vague maps of what is under the soil. These glorified metal-detectors include magnetometers, measurers of soil resistivity, and sundry other ways of passing energy through the ground. If funds do not run to this, probes can be pushed into the ground at frequent intervals. Failure to check out a site adequately led one British archaeologist a few years ago to dig his way down into the London Underground.

On any dig there are a number of standard characters you will encounter.

The **Excavation Director** is rather like a general. He (it is most often a he) plans the overall strategy but leaves all the hard work to the infantry, dealing only with the paperwork: supplies, accounts, permits, begging letters, and so forth.

The **Site Supervisors** or officers – often graduate students – act as liaisons between the general and the infantry, and generally make the most of their lofty status. They occasionally have some idea of what is being done at the site and why.

The **Diggers** or infantry – undergraduates, local convicts or civilian volunteers – are the cannon fodder, usually providing all the sweaty labour and kept in a state of blissful ignorance about what they are doing and why. Amazingly, some even pay money to be treated this way. Their basic task often appears to be to move dirt from one place to another, occasionally sieving it into different sizes before dumping it.

Bluffers should know that much of the time little real digging occurs: the dirt is loosened with a trowel and brushed aside, which is a good deal slower. In most parts of the world the shifting is done with shovels, buckets and wheel-barrows. In Japan, however, where mechanisation is rampant, even minor archaeological sites have the dirt removed on a series of overlapping conveyor belts to the spoilheap.

Other exciting chores include washing the finds (mostly bits of stone, bone or pot), writing tiny numbers on them, and drawing, bagging and cataloguing them. In the past all the information was collected in excavation notebooks, together with exact measurements of the objects' precise position in the site. It did not matter too much if the notebooks were accurate – comforting news for the digging bluffer – as there are few things more mindnumbing than trying to make sense of someone else's excavation notes, and the books were usually never looked at again. Today, on advanced digs, these data are tapped directly into computers, which not only means that the machines produce all the site plans far more easily and quickly than students, but also that the more irrelevant and useless data can be ignored even more rapidly than before.

Use of computers, of course, also makes the dig appear to be at the very forefront of modern technology – never mind that they are only as useful and accurate as the information keyed into them in the first place, which in turn depends on the quality and vigilance of the excavators as well as of the computer operators. Computer printouts, maps and diagrams make your reports look terrifically impressive and professional, and have the extra advantage that they usually deter readers from examining your evidence very closely.

Some directors – probably those who had a deservedly lonely childhood – object to diggers chatting as they work. This makes an already dull job unbearable. Faced with days of unremittingly tedious labour of this kind, it is little wonder that most diggers secretly long to make an exciting find, a body perhaps or even some treasure. This is not advisable, however, as it can lead to visits by looters, or complaints and threats from local people who object to their ancestors being disturbed, and of course there is the ever-present possibility of curses.

Diggers need strong knees in order to cope with long hours working bent legged on planks or subsoils: being a Catholic or Japanese is useful training here.

Sites can generally be divided into two types:

1. Wetland (full of soggy wood)
2. Dryland (no soggy wood at all).

Wetland archaeologists have a superiority complex as they are able to find the kind of perishable stuff that has normally disintegrated on dryland sites. They risk developing trench-foot.

Dryland archaeologists have a far less messy time of it, and only risk pneumoconiosis (if the site is *really* dry).

Work on either kind of site should help you get a tan (not in Britain), build up muscles, and lose weight (not in France).

Some people hope that a dig will be like a Club 18-30 holiday, and many are; but there is usually a ranking system in operation, with the most attractive diggers aiming for the director first, the supervisors next, and fellow diggers only as a last resort. A few French directors are notorious for attracting American 'groupies' to their digs.

Never admit to someone of higher rank that this is your first dig, or that you don't know what you are doing. Apart from being as potentially embarrassing

21

as confessing to virginity, such an admission will lead to your being given all the most menial tasks which practised hands try to avoid, e.g:
– digging latrines
– making the coffee
or both.

Your equipment and clothes should give the appearance of being well used, and you should assume an air of fake self-confidence and casualness about the whole business.

Fundamental Laws

There are a few fundamental laws in archaeological excavation with which you should be familiar:

1. The most interesting part of the site will be under your spoilheap, or at least outside the area you choose to dig.

2. The most important find will turn up on the last day or when you're pressed for time and funds (this is known as the Howard Carter law – he found Tutankhamun just before his funding was to be cut off by Lord Carnarvon).

3. Finding anything worthwhile will involve extending your dig, and in any case will not be what you were looking for.

4. If in doubt, hack it out.

5. Only falsify your data where absolutely necessary: this is for the most cynical bluffers who take confidence from the knowledge that every site is unique, excavation destroys it, and so nobody can ever redo your work and prove you wrong.

Useful things to take on an excavation:

- Camping equipment
- Scruffy old clothing, including T-shirt marked 'Archaeologists do it in holes'
- A pointing trowel (in France a bent screwdriver is preferred, which tells you something about the French). Make sure it looks old and battered enough to pass yourself off as a veteran.
- Insect repellent
- Insurance (in case a trench collapses on you)
- Condoms
- A bottle opener and corkscrew.

Survey

The principal 'active' alternative to excavation these days is surface survey. This involves systematically walking a site or landscape, scanning it for archaeological traces of all kinds – walls, structures, bits of stone or pottery, etc. These are then carefully plotted on maps, and information conjured up from the patterns. Survey fans are fiercely proud of their type of work, being conscious of the fact that excavators consider survey a poor relation, and that excavation is the only way to be *sure* what lies beneath the surface. In fact each method has different strengths: excavation tells you a lot about a small area, survey tells you a little about a big area.

Survey is pretty good for bluffing, because objects are often not even collected, but simply have their presence and location noted. So every survey is unique and can never be repeated exactly. Consequently, nobody can check your facts, and the only way to challenge your claims is to excavate the whole area of your survey.

Survey used to be considered a second-best, undertaken where permission, funds or personnel for a dig were not available. But today it has been realized that survey is faster and a lot less expensive than digging, certainly less destructive, and requires virtually no equipment other than maps, students and stout footwear.

Useful things to take on a survey:
- Camping equipment
- Scruffy old clothing, including T-shirt marked 'Archaeologists do it systematically all over the landscape'
- Floppy hat (if abroad; in Britain, an umbrella or anorak)
- Foot powder
- A compass
- Sting relief
- Local phrase book (check wording for 'Beware of the bull', 'Electrified fence', 'Minefield', etc.)

Rescue

Some people are professional diggers, attached to units run by regional authorities. Most of their work involves rapid excavation of sites that are threatened with imminent destruction by various causes. It therefore entails little overall strategy: the stuff is dug up for the sake of it, to preserve it for posterity. Their colleagues in academia who claim to do planned research excavations often scoff at this kind of catch-all procedure. Naturally the bluffer should praise Rescue Archaeology if faced with a researcher, and vice versa.

THE SPECIALISTS

Something has to be done with all the data gathered in the field, and this is where a wide range of people, many of them outside archaeology itself, are called upon to do their stuff.

Stone Tool Experts

These individuals are responsible for putting bits of worked stone into different categories according to shape and style, and trying to figure out what they were used for. This has become a little easier recently by looking at wear patterns and residues on their working edges through powerful microscopes – human blood has even been detected on some prehistoric stone tools, which suggests that some makers were as clumsy as modern experimenters.

Bluffers should avoid bad jokes about 'chips off the old block', having a 'knap', or living on a diet of core 'n' flakes.

Few specialists are less envigorating than those who have devoted their lives to bits of stone, but they are run a close second by:

Pottery Experts

It may take a crackpot to love a cracked pot, but bits of pottery (or 'sherds' or 'shards') are almost as numerous and as indestructible as stone tools in archaeology, so it is lucky that some people choose this line of work. Trying to reconstruct shattered pots is a frustrating and delicate task, like a 3-D jigsaw, especially if there is a piece missing or several left over. Those who do not wish to be thrown by making a slip need to have an even temper.

Zoologists

Archaeologists often depend on zoologists to identify the animal remains they exhume. Bone experts have things easier than their botanical colleagues (see below), as bone fragments are bigger, better preserved and more readily identifiable than plant remains. Hence a growing number of archaeologists feel able to tackle this job, calling themselves 'zooarchaeologists' or 'archaeozoologists'. The bluffer will, of course, prefer the alternative version to that used.

Some even specialise further, in fish bones, or bird bones, or rodents, or in mollusc shells: snails are a particularly easy subject to keep up with.

Botanists

Archaeologists rely on botanists to identify any bits of vegetation they may dig up (wood, seeds, nuts, grains), no matter how soggy or charred these may be. The botanists often extract the material in a gunge, after putting sediment from the site through a flotation machine or a wet sieve. They then have to peer down microscopes at this ancient muesli and do their best to make sense of it.

Things are a little more interesting if the mixture comes from a stomach. Tollund Man, the preserved Iron Age body of the first century B.C., which was found in a Danish peat bog with a noose round his neck, had a number of plant remains in his stomach, indicating that his last meal was a kind of gruel comprising seeds and grains. On eating a reconstruction of this tasteless mush, Mortimer Wheeler announced that Tollund Man had probably committed suicide, if that was the sort of cooking he got at home.

Some botanists specialise in the study of pollen (the accomplished bluffer will refer to them as palynologists). Pollen grains survive amazingly well, and can reveal a great deal about past vegetation and climate by showing what was growing in different places and periods. The study of pollen is, however, a very taxing discipline, and one that gets right up some people's noses.

Coprolite Analysts

Coprolites are fossil faeces, and specimens from animals and humans may be found in archaeological sites, especially very dry ones or waterlogged ones. They represent the most direct evidence for what was actually eaten, so unfortunately their contents need to be extracted and identified. A small number of intrepid experts around the world know how to treat the coprolites with chemicals so that they regain their original form, texture and even their smell.

One American specialist is said to be capable of recognizing some substances in treated coprolites (such as liquorice) from the odour alone. These experts are generally and undeservedly given a wide berth by other scholars, since their work comprises such close encounters of the turd kind.

Dating

Scientists are responsible for the invaluable service of providing archaeology with an absolute chronology. Archaeologists give them bits of charcoal, bone, pottery and so forth, and the boffins work their magic and tell the archaeologists how old these objects are. The physicists must feel very popular, as people keep asking them for dates; meeting Physics has transformed archaeology's life.

Bluffers only need know the rudiments of a couple of major methods with impressive names:

1. Dendrochronology

Trees grow by annual rings, and since the thickness of each ring varies with the climatic conditions of the year (rich growth in favourable years, etc.) an unbroken series of rings can be built up and extended back for centuries by 'overlapping' identical sequences preserved on modern and ancient timbers. After that, any bit of wood found in the area can have its rings checked against the master sequence and its precise age established. This is the archaeological version of calculating by logs.

2. Thermoluminescence

There is no need to know exactly how this works. Just be aware that it is mainly used to date pottery. It appears that you can figure out how long ago an object was heated up by measuring the amount of light it gives off when reheated. It is not thought to work for left-overs, but you can date food by:

3. Radiocarbon dating

This method is used on organic substances, and measures the minuscule amount of the radioactive isotope Carbon 14 left in them – after an organism's death, the amount of C14 it contains diminishes steadily, together with the volume of junk mail it receives.

Radiocarbon dates are a paradise for bluffers. They comprise a figure followed by a plus-or-minus sign and another figure: for example, 2450 ± 80 BP means that the age of the object in years may be between 2530 and 2370 years before the present – but there is only a 66 per cent chance that it lies within this span.

Few people can remember radiocarbon dates with any accuracy, so you can usually get away with any figure that sounds in the right order of magnitude. If challenged, say yours is a calibrated figure (i.e. corrected because of the various complicated ways in which Radiocarbon is inaccurate). There have been many attempts to produce standardised 'calibration curves' (by dating objects and tree rings of known age and seeing how wrong C14 is in each case), and each is different.

When confronted with a Radiocarbon date, the bluffer can resort to several ploys:

a) Question its accuracy (if uncalibrated), or that of its calibration.
b) Enquire what material the date was produced from – dates from shell, for example, are notoriously inaccurate.
c) Point out that a single Radiocarbon date is not much use anyway – these days only a whole series of them is considered reliable.

In addition, any date can be called into question simply by casting doubt on the way in which the sample was collected, and suggesting that it may have been contaminated in some way. Very few archaeological dates can stand up to this sort of scrutiny, and your opponent will have to yield to your rigorous scientific standards or risk looking either dangerously dogmatic or sloppy.

Interpretation

There are two basic trends in archaeology of which the bluffer should be aware.

1. The dates for various inventions (such as pottery) or events (e.g. the arrival of humans in Australia) are constantly being pushed back.
2. The places of origin of different archaeological

features, including people themselves, shift around the globe as new discoveries are made. As Breuil said of human origins, 'The cradle of humanity is on casters.'

So the art of interpreting archaeological evidence is to leave yourself room for manoeuvre in the light of future discovery.

The shortcomings of archaeological interpretation should be readily apparent: indeed, it has been described as 'the recovery of unobservable behaviour patterns from indirect traces in bad samples'. The astute bluffer can drive home the point with a parable about some archaeologist far in the future trying to make sense of a late 20th century site – buildings marked with golden arches would be identified as places of worship where ritual meals were prepared; the main deity is clearly a mouse in red pants and white gloves (its image is found everywhere, especially on clothing); and the Coca Cola bottle would be a phallic symbol or a female figurine according to the interpreter's predilections.

Curses

It is popularly believed – thanks to movies, comic strips and tabloids – that archaeologists who disturb tombs or sacred sites fall prey to dire curses. The most famous case is that of the tomb of Tutankhamun, since Lord Carnarvon (who financed the work) died a few months after the tomb was discovered in 1922. Bluffers should scoff at this belief, suggesting that Tutankhamun might have devised a more spectacular death for Carnarvon than falling victim to pneumonia (in fact it is likely that his death was due to inhalation,

30

in a passage leading to the tomb, of a fungus in the dried dust from bat droppings).

You can also point out that Howard Carter, who actually found and stripped the tomb and disturbed the body, died a natural death some 17 years later.

Many deaths following archaeological disturbance of tombs and other sites can in fact be attributed to a more mundane cause: archaeology is a dirty business, sifting through old rubbish and decayed organic matter. It would be surprising if there were not occasional germs and spores lurking somewhere in the debris, and since archaeologists are not known for cleanliness they may well eat their on-site snacks with hands that are less than spotless. Excavators therefore recommend tetanus shots and carbolic soap.

A variety of other curses can afflict archaeologists, especially in the field:

1) Colds, chills or worse (especially in Britain)
2) Blisters, sunstroke, collapsing trenches
3) The runs (known as Montezuma's revenge)
4) Angry locals
5) Site-looters
6) Lack of finds (the 'barren site' curse) and, worst of all,
7) Running out of alcohol.

A different kind of modern curse is the rise of an enthusiastic army of amateurs with metal-detectors. For some reason these people get their excitement from digging up old scraps of metal or coins, and an even bigger and more understandable thrill out of finding valuable hoards of treasure. If faced with such people, the archaeological bluffer should preach patronisingly against their ever touching known archaeological sites, and urge them to restrict their activities to shore-lines and spoilheaps (though most archaeologists would, in fact, prefer them to work in minefields).

If confronting a professional archaeologist, however, the bluffer will speak up on behalf of the responsible and careful metal-detector enthusiast, while taking pains to condemn the majority. Archaeologists can get quite over-wrought about this question of digging up metal, and wish people would leave it to rust in peace until it can be excavated properly in its full archaeological context.

Many feel that anyone who selfishly plunders a piece of the past (whether a site-looter or an archaeologist who fails to publish a report) has stolen something irreplaceable from all humanity. It is advisable therefore, even if you have a pronounced sense of the absurd, to appear to take the past very seriously. After all it's the only one we've got.

Fakes

People are extremely easy to fool, and archaeologists are no exception. Over the years, great numbers of them have fallen prey to unscrupulous individuals and have believed in the authenticity of fakes.

You should know that one of the earliest known fakers was an Englishman, Edward Simpson (1815-c.1875), ultimately known as **Flint Jack** and also, less felicitously, as Fossil Willie. He became a prolific forger of flint tools, ancient implements and pottery, often passing them off to experts and amateurs alike as genuine specimens. More of a practical joker than a crook, he just liked taking people for a ride, and eventually took to giving public displays of his expertise. Flint Jack was something of an 'archaeologist manqué', as he was extremely scruffy, had a terrible weakness for drink, and died in poverty.

Controversy still rages in France over a site called **Glozel**, dug in the 1920s, which contained a set of amazing and obvious fakes, supposedly showing that Ice Age carvings, Bronze Age pots and Near Eastern inscribed clay tablets all co-existed in this one spot near Vichy. Yet a few archaeologists are still reluctant to dismiss the site, and many non-archaeologists still uphold it as an example of blinkered archaeology not wanting to face up to awkward facts and an unknown civilisation. One American has even 'deciphered' the Glozel tablets, and claims they show the place was a bazaar selling ointments, amulets, and devices to ensure sexual potency.

The most famous fakery occurred in England in 1912 when **Piltdown Man**, a 'missing link', was trumpeted as the earliest Englishman.

It says much for the archaeologists' lack of humour that they still did not smell a rat when Piltdown produced a bone implement shaped like a cricket bat.

Pseudo-archaeology

Archaeologists have long been accustomed to dealing with harmless individuals obsessed by the fate of the Ten Lost Tribes of Israel, the location of the lost continent of Mu, or the bizarre idea that everything in the British landscape can be joined together along straight lines or in the form of signs of the zodiac. Most museums and other such institutions are pestered by their share of cranks who believe that Atlantis was in Glasgow or that the number of blocks in the Great Pyramid is mysteriously equal to the number of words in the Bible. One man, however, has taken this kind of thing to new heights (or depths, depending on your viewpoint), and in a book like this deserves a section of his own as the epitome of archaeological bluffing.

An obscure Swiss hotel manager, twice convicted of

fraud and embezzlement, **Erich von Däniken** in 1968 wrote a book called *Chariots of the Gods* which, together with its very similar successors, sold over 25 million copies in 32 countries – probably more than all archaeology books combined.

His ideas were not original, but have become associated with his name. Put simply, they ascribe anything in the human past that looks difficult or bizarre (big monuments, enigmatic drawings) to visitors from outer space. Regardless of whether he believed this 'ancient astronaut' concept, he made it far better known and more widely accepted than any archaeological theory, the ultimate achievement for a bluffer.

Few scholars have bothered to write books to counter the theory, partly because they felt it beneath their dignity and partly because such books never sell. As it would be unethical to let these falsehoods go unchallenged, you should have a few basic facts at hand – but only a few, as the typical von Däniken fan is the kind of person whose lips move while reading. You will not need to study his books in depth: a mere skim through one of them, or just the picture captions, will suffice to show you his approach and his uses of sleight-of-hand.

If, on the other hand, faced with someone who is already anti-von Däniken, you are forced to find something positive to say about him, stress that his books are useful aids for teaching students how *not* to write, and how to recognize:

– false logic
– tricks of presentation
– blatant distortions of the truth, and
– sly selection of facts.

Then swiftly admit, before being challenged, that many archaeological texts can serve the same purpose.

ARCHAEOLOGY IN PRINT

Although there are now innumerable books and journals devoted to archaeology, only a small percentage are owed to a desire to disseminate knowledge to colleagues, let alone to the public that usually footed the bill for the work. The vast majority of archaeological publications are produced with one aim in mind: self advancement.

When applying for jobs or research funds, an archaeologist has to supply a list of publications with the Curriculum Vitae, and an impressive list can make a big difference to promotion prospects: never mind the quality, feel the length. Size does matter in academic circles.

Since few archaeologists manage to keep up a stream of innovative and varied studies, most employ a great deal of bluff in this area. It may entail publishing reams of meaningless abstraction with no possible application or relevance to the real world (see Theoretical Archaeology); or, more commonly, endlessly recycling the same piece of work: this is known as the 'Enid Blyton Syndrome', and enables one to achieve a massive list of publications with minimum effort. As long as the titles and journals are different, you are home and dry – referees cannot read everything, and most papers are read by only a few people.

So, most of the time, this bluff is easy to carry off. Indeed, it is self-perpetuating, as the more you publish the easier it becomes to get published; and anyone outside the system or with something new and original to say will often be refereed by the Blytonians and thus weeded out. It also means that, at conferences, everyone already knows what everyone else is going to say, so can spend more time propping up the bar.

Papers usually have to be given at conferences in order to get grants to attend. You also need to bluff the funding agency into believing that the conference is of enormous importance to your subject. In fact, however, little new is ever said at such events, and their main functions are for socialising, gossiping, philandering, job hunting, and generally proving that you're still around.

Books are a more complex problem than papers, as they usually take some time to reasearch and write. Once again, however, there are some notable shortcuts for the expert bluffer.

1. Learn to waffle at great length (see Theoretical Archaeology).

2. Synthesise the work of others (stealing from one author is plagiarism, but from many is research). Or better still,

3. Synthesise your own work by lumping together some of your old articles between hard covers.

The lucky few who bluff their way to fame will even find that publishers are keen to pay money to put their names on the covers of books to which they have contributed only a token preface.

Another crafty way to get your name on the front of a book is to edit it: this simply entails writing to a number of people and asking if they would like to contribute a chapter or a paper to a prestigious new volume. Most are so flattered to be asked, and so desperate to add another item to their publications list, that they rush to comply, and, hey presto, a book of other people's hard work comes out under your name. One or two archaeologists on both sides of the Atlantic are so practised at this dodge that they bring out at least one edited book per year. They may be packed with hot air, but quality of content is irrelevant to the perception of productivity.

Ruses

Hedging
One basic rule for bluffers in archaeological publishing is to avoid dogmatism, and to fill your work with 'maybe', 'perhaps', and 'possibly'. This enables you to make an orderly and dignified retreat in case of attack or being proved wrong.

Obfuscating
Another way to sidestep criticism is to make your prose so obscure and tortuous that nobody, including yourself, is quite sure at the end of it what you have been saying. This smokescreen effect, particularly common in theoretical work, is very useful when it turns out that you were wrong, or new finds alter the situation: you can simply claim that you were misunderstood and that you said nothing of the kind.

Padding
Another ruse in print is to include lots of lists and tables, which nobody will ever bother to check or read through, but which serve to make your work seem scholarly and thorough. Similarly, some authors, many of them French, put a long bibliography at the end, containing numerous impressive sources – most of which are never actually referred to in the text. It's just window-dressing, but very effective since it is unlikely that anyone will read the entire work and notice the absences.

Non-publication

Some archaeologists get away for years, even decades, without publishing anything of note. This is more serious if they are thereby withholding, from colleagues and the world at large, information which they have dug up or otherwise obtained. Many are the cases around the world, involving some very famous sites, but instead of ostracising the individuals concerned, archaeologists generally treat them with the utmost courtesy and only mutter about them behind their backs.

There are a number of basic reasons for non-publication:

1. Laziness, lethargy or complacency (primarily among those with tenured jobs who therefore don't have to worry about having their output assessed).
2. Incompetence. This takes many forms: some can hardly string two sentences together, let alone produce an accurate report on a piece of work. Others are congenitally untidy, so notes and even finds get lost in the stratigraphy that builds up in their offices and laboratories. One or two have even been known to be so absent-minded that they leave manuscripts, notes and irreplaceable finds on trains.
3. Terror. Some are so thin-skinned that the very thought of laying themselves open to criticism is torture. Of course, the fact that they don't publish is also attacked, but this is considered the lesser of the two evils in a subject where you are guaranteed to be torn to shreds by someone whatever you do.
4. Being too busy. New lecturers tend to be given the heaviest teaching load, as well as all the jobs nobody else can stand, such as serving on library

committees, marking exam papers and conducting outings to museums. Others are simply too pre-occupied with building their careers to pay any attention to little matters like ethics.

5. The conveyor belt. Many archaeologists, amaz-ingly, are permitted to keep digging or researching without publishing anything on what they have already done. This soon builds up a huge backlog of data and finds, most of which will never be analysed and processed, let alone published. As a phenomenon it gives an illusion of constant activity. In reality it is the best ruse of all.

Very few archaeologists have ever been known to admit their mistakes, in print at any rate. Even in published retractions, they generally state that their original position was correct, but that circumstances have changed. Thus criticism of their earlier work can be deflected by the comment 'That's what I thought at the time, but I've moved on since then.' You can never actually pin them down to explaining clearly how they view the problem at present. Backtracking and U-turns are all too easy to those practised at this kind of manoeuvre.

Bluffers must always give the impression of being very well read in the subject, not only in their writings but also in conversation. If asked whether you have read some new book, you can plead poverty and claim to be waiting for the paperback (few serious archaeology books ever come out in paperback), and thus steer talk into the ever-worsening problem of grossly-overpriced texts. Another effective ploy if asked about a specific book or article is to express enthusiasm, and say that you are terribly busy but dying to read it as soon as your limited spare time permits: then turn the tables by asking your companion's opinion.

SOME NAMES TO KNOW

If, at a party, you are asked what you do, and you confess that you are working on a typology of clay pipes dug up around Stoke Poges, you are not going to enthral your audience for more than 2.5 seconds. All aspiring archaeological bluffers therefore need to know something about the more exotic people and places that *do* interest others, preferably those which remain enigmatic or controversial and to which there is no complete answer. Here are a few to choose from:

Stonehenge

One of the very few British archaeological sites that the whole world has heard of, this unique structure on Salisbury Plain comprises a 'henge' (a circular area bounded by earth banks and a ditch) with huge stones ('megaliths') set upright inside it. The biggest stones even have horizontal slabs set on top of them (two uprights and a lintel form a 'trilithon'), using a mortise and tenon system – i.e. bumps on the uprights fit into corresponding hollows in the lintels. It is not known exactly how the horizontal stones could be fitted there, though visiting astronauts are unlikely to have been recruited.

The biggest stones (sarsens) are local, but the bluestones (which are actually bluish with pink flecks) are thought to have been brought from Wales – perhaps there was discount there for bulk purchase. Excavators have divided the site's development, spanning a period from about 3000 to 1100 B.C., into a whole series of phases (I, II, IIIa,b,c) which nobody can remember (IIIb or not IIIb? That is the question). If asked about these, you can neatly sidestep the issue by claiming to disagree with the sequence and explaining that you are waiting for the full excavation report to appear in order to assess the evidence for yourself.

Stonehenge is generally thought to be a ritual site (anything in archaeology with no obvious function is classed as ritual). It clearly has some astronomical significance as it is aligned on the midsummer sunrise. However, it predates the Druids by many centuries, and there is no evidence for a link either with their religion or with human sacrifice. This does not stop a bunch of people in white nightgowns turning up there every June to perform some pseudo-Druidic ceremonies.

In recent years Stonehenge has also become the focus of a midsummer invasion by hippies, who presumably venerate it as the earliest rock group, and who gather there to give thanks for the rising sun and their Social Security cheques.

Carnac

A collection of prehistoric standing stones in Brittany, and not to be confused with Karnak (a huge temple in Egypt), they run in rows for miles across the landscape, looking like the endless vistas of termite mounds in northern Australia. Bluffers should, however, use such similes carefully, or impressionable listeners will automatically assume that the Carnac megaliths were erected by a party of homesick Aborigines.

Sites like Carnac are bread and butter to the bluffer since nobody has the faintest idea what they were. They are as usual, assumed to have been ritual, and inevitably thought to have some astronomical function, but basically your guess is as good as anyone else's. You should know that these standing stones are called menhirs. If this brings up the *Asterix* books, point out that, while funny, the books are archaeologically bogus because they bring prehistoric megaliths

41

thousands of years forward to Roman times. This may brand you a spoilsport, but will confirm your credentials as a stickler for factual accuracy.

The Terracotta Army
The biggest find of recent years, it was, as usual, made not by archaeologists but by Chinese peasants drilling for water. What they found near Xian (pronounced She-an) turned out to be thousands of lifesize clay figures of soldiers and horses arranged in ranks. They were made to guard, in death, the emperor Qin Shihuangdi (3rd century B.C.), who is buried under a huge mound some distance away. This strange practice was, at least, an improvement on slaughtering people to do the job in the afterlife: in any case, who could you get to massacre your whole army?

The troops were clearly well equipped and armed, demonstrating that the Chinese army had not yet gone to pot by this time. Anxious archaeologists are wondering if they can also expect a terracotta navy to turn up – did great emperor have fleet of clay?

Nazca
An intriguing mystery, this desert in Peru is covered by thousands of straight lines that go for miles, running parallel or criss-crossing, and by scores of huge outline drawings of animals, birds, fish, spiders, etc. They were made centuries ago by moving stones aside to reveal the lighter earth beneath, and only make sense from the air. Maria Reiche, a German mathematician, has spent decades trying to prove that they have an astronomical function; it goes without saying that they are generally considered ritual. Von Däniken insists the site is a kind of airport for flying saucers; others propose the Nazcans had the knowledge and technology to go up in balloons (like many archae-

ologists, they knew a lot about hot air). Bluffers might try suggesting that the Nazca people were just extremely tall. There is no evidence for this, but there isn't any for astronauts or balloons either.

Aztecs and Incas

Many people, including most beginning students, find it hard to remember which of these two peoples lived in Peru and which in Mexico, and whether they were destroyed by Cortes or by Pizarro. Bluffers can keep these basic facts at their fingertips by recalling that:

- Inca and Peru both have four letters, Peru and Pizarro both begin with a P.
- Aztecs, Mexico and Cortes all have six letters.

The devastation of these two great civilisations by the Spanish lust for gold is one of the most tragic episodes in human history. Some believe that the devastation of much of Spain by British holidaymakers' lust for sun, sea and sangria is a delayed divine retribution.

The Incas made impressive temples and forts of enormous blocks beautifully fitted together (though probably not by passing astronauts). They had heaps of gold, but no writing: they used knotted string instead, and even Champollion would have had his work cut out to decipher those. Their most famous site is Machu Picchu (pronounced Matchoo Pitchoo), which sounds like someone sneezing.

The Aztecs are associated with big temple platforms like pyramids, and with sacrificing thousands of enemies in order to feed the ravenous appetite of their gods. If pressed on the topic, you can deflect questions by mentioning other groups in Mesoamerica (*not* Mexico, please) such as the Toltecs, Mixtecs, Zapotecs, Chichimecs and Maya. Only a New World specialist would know how all these fit together spatially and chronologically, and as such specialists are very thin on the ground outside America, you are pretty safe to waffle at will. The most famous Mesoamerican site to drop into conversation is Chichén Itzá, which also sounds like someone sneezing.

If you find you get Machu Picchu and Chichén Itzá mixed up, figure out your own way to remember which is which – we can't hand you everything on a plate.

Easter Island
Most people are familiar with the gigantic stone heads dotted around this tiny speck of land in the Pacific (though bluffers will dismiss talk of the 'heads' since the statues actually include the torso, but have become buried up to the neck over the years). Unfortunately, most people are also familiar with von Däniken's claims that the volcanic rock here is too hard to be carved by stone tools, and that in any case there were no trees to provide rollers and levers to move these monsters. Consequently it must have been (surprise, surprise) astronauts again.

In fact, the rock is exceptionally soft and easy to carve, there are thousands of hammer-stones and hundreds of unfinished statues still in the quarry, and there is ample evidence from pollen and other botanical remains that the whole island was originally covered in big palm trees, admirably suitable for use as rollers, etc. _

Bluffers should try to steer conversations about Easter Island (always use the Islanders' own names for it, Rapa Nui and Navel of the World) away from the statues to the amazing rock-carvings of vulvas. In Easter Island culture, the clitoris was deliberately lengthened from an early age, and girls were expected to straddle two rocks to display them to priests at certain ceremonies. The longest were honoured by being immortalised in stone, and their proud owners would get the best warriors as husbands. Modern women might share a similar ambition, but would probably feel that going to those lengths to achieve it is stretching the point.

Australia
Australian archaeology as a whole is a valuable area for the bluffer as it's only been underway for 25 years, and hardly anyone outside Australia knows anything about it. Dazzle your audience by mentioning such sites as Lake Mungo, Kutikina, Kow Swamp and Beginners' Luck Cave.

It is also one of the richest areas for rock art, with thousands of sites and millions of motifs. Some sites are still sacred to the Aborigines who give them evocative names such as Darangingnarri ('Walk over to woman with open legs.').

Fields of Specialisation

There are a wide range of interesting sub-disciplines within archaeology on which one can choose to concentrate. A bluffer need only be an 'expert' in whichever subject the other person knows nothing about.

Egyptology
Not the liveliest branch of the subject (it is, after all, characterised by the Book of the Dead) this field nevertheless remains popular with the public because of its impressive and photogenic monuments, its mysteries, picture-writing, strange gods and spectacular treasures. Most movies with an archaeological theme are set in Egypt, and usually involve mummies and

curses. So if you want to bluff your way in archaeology you clearly need to know a bit about this civilisation.

It is simple to bluff in Egyptology as most non-archaeologists have heard of only a handful of people (Tutankhamun, Cleopatra, and perhaps Cheops and Nefertiti) and sites (Valley of the Kings, the Pyramids, Abu Simbel), so you can dazzle them without much difficulty by mentioning a couple of obscure pharaohs such as Sesostris or Sheshonk. Should you be faced with someone who has been on a tour of Egypt, you do not need to show any expertise at all – just let them ramble on at length about their experiences and impressions.

In order to demonstrate an intimate knowledge of the less familiar aspects of ancient Egyptian life, you could mention the (absolutely genuine) British Museum papyrus that provides the recipe for a love potion to win a woman's love: the man has to mix some dandruff from a murdered person's scalp with some barley grains and apple pips, then add a little of his own blood and semen, and finally the blood of a tick from a black dog. This mixture, if slipped into the lady's drink, should have devastating consequences. Another winning formula, designed to make a woman enjoy love-making, was to rub the foam from a stallion's mouth into one's own 'obelisk'.

If challenged to translate some hieroglyphics, make up something dull and religious that sounds plausible, and your audience will be satisfied: for example 'O Lord of the Two Kingdoms, Beloved of Nut, the Divine Mother, and of Re, thy enemies prostrate themselves before thy all-conquering chariot'. Another particularly effective bluff is to talk in terms of dynasties – 'that probably dates to the early 13th dynasty' – since everyone will be impressed and nobody will dare to admit they don't know what you're talking about. Even most non-Egyptological archaeologists won't have a clue about fitting dates (much less pharaohs) to dynasties. Tutankhamun, incidentally, was of the 18th dynasty, Sesostris the 12th, and Sheshonk the 22nd.

The Near East
Exactly the same applies to Near Eastern archaeology, since only specialists can remember the difference between Sumerians, Babylonians, Akkadians, Assyrians, Hittites and sundry others. The merest reference to the 3rd dynasty of Ur should establish the depth of your knowledge, while a mention of (King) Nabonidus will clinch your expertise.

The only features of Near Eastern archaeology that you need be familiar with are the royal tombs of Ur with their gold treasures; the great mound-sites known as 'tells'; and the enormous stepped towers called ziggurats (meaning mountain peaks). The most famous of these was the tower of Babel (Babylon): its construction, according to the Bible, led to disaster, which proves that ziggurats are bad for your health.

Bluffers should also be aware that the Dead Sea Scrolls comprise thousands of fragments of ancient Hebrew books, about 2000 years old, that were found by shepherds tossing a stone into a cave near the Dead Sea, and that as word spread about the importance of the finds they were able to get a price of £1 per square inch for them.

The accomplished bluffer will take care to differentiate serious Biblical archaeologists, who investigate sites in the Bible lands, from the fanatics who take the Bible as Gospel and keep trying to find bits of Noah's Ark on Mount Ararat.

Decipherment

A dying art, as most early scripts have now been deciphered, this is now largely restricted to figuring out what a doctor has written on your prescription, or to secretaries trying to transcribe the scrawl they have been handed. However, in the last couple of centuries it was all the rage, with many kinds of brainteasing puzzles to be cracked around the world.

Jean François Champollion (1790–1832) was one of the best codebreakers. He wrote a book at the age of 12, and by 13 was reading Arabic, Syriac and Coptic, so one can imagine what an insufferable little prodigy he must have been. In 1808 he started work on the Rosetta Stone (which had identical texts in Egyptian scripts and in Greek) and by 1822 had mastered the decipherment of hieroglyphics. Most other decipherers were less fortunate and, instead of having a handy crib of that type, had to start from scratch.

One ancient script that merits the attention of bluffers is that of the Indus civilisation, since it has still not been cracked, so whatever you say about it nobody knows whether you're right or wrong. An even more obscure one is the Rongo Rongo script of Easter Island which only survives as engraved characters on 29 pieces of wood. The modern islanders have occasionally been asked to translate these texts, but tend to come up with something different every time, which means they are pretty good bluffers themselves.

Rock Art

One of the jollier aspects of archaeology, this entails the location, recording and study of ancient carvings and paintings on rocks. Those involved need to be tough (much of the art is in deep caves, high mountains or very hot areas) and include many of the most eccentric characters one could wish to meet.

In the absence of the original artists it is impossible to know very much about these pictures, and this is therefore an ideal area for bluffing. Better still, many places are almost inaccessible: for example, caves tend to contain sharp stalactites, crevasses, deep water, guano, mosquitoes, and even, in some parts of the world, killer bees. One cave in the Dordogne, mercifully not open to the public, lies beneath the village of Domme and has always served as its sewer. The entrance is through a coal bunker in someone's back yard, the cave stinks, and it is wise not to examine too closely the sticky goo that has to be negotiated. Occasionally, during the visit, another load is flushed into the cave from a house above. The purpose of the exercise is to see a single, mediocre Ice Age drawing of a bison. Few specialists return for a second viewing.

Underwater Archaeology

Excavating on land is hard enough, but some people like to make things extra tricky for themselves, and working underwater is the archaeological equivalent of standing up in a hammock. Bluffers can point out with wry amusement that the best known practitioner is aptly named George Bass.

Most of the work is done on the seabed, in harbours, or in lakes, but occasionally it can also involve unusual sites such as the great 'cenote' or sacred well of the Maya at Chichén Itzá into which great quantities of gold and jade objects, and (female) virgins according to Spanish accounts, were thrown as sacrifices. You may safely claim that the latter cannot be correct since work by divers and dredgers in the 40ft of water and 10ft of muck at the bottom has shown that many of the skeletal remains belong to men and children.

Underwater archaeologists get very excited about ship designs and cargoes, topics that leave terrestrial colleagues fairly cold unless they find something particularly old or unusual or well preserved. The land-lubbers probably harbour a grudge because they cannot see all these sites for themselves except on film. So occasionally the underwater archaeologists raise an entire ship to the surface and finish the study there. This was done recently with a collection of sodden timbers that used to be the Tudor ship *Mary Rose*.

The *Mary Rose* sank only a short distance from port, which does not say much for British shipbuilding even in those days, and bluffers can stress the fact that archaeological evidence suggests the crew had already started playing dice before the voyage was properly underway, which might be seen as the 16th century equivalent of leaving the bow doors open.

Urban Archaeology
Much work has been done on archaeological sites within towns and cities in recent decades – partly through a growing interest in the urban past, but more often through sheer necessity as more and more demolition and construction goes on, giving archaeologists a brief chance between operations to look at what lies under the chosen site. If you find brick foundations, soggy leather shoes, glazed potsherds, clay pipes and endless quantities of chicken bones a source of great fascination, then this is the field for you. Occasionally the town may stretch back beyond the medieval period, and then you can also delve into the glories of Viking cesspits and Roman sewers.

The great advantages of urban archaeology are:
1. You will probably be seen on local television.
2. You are never far from home, supplies or medical assistance.
3. You don't have to camp out.
4. There are pubs within easy reach.

The disadvantages are that there are always lots of passers-by gawping at you and asking irritating questions, and even worse, your family and friends can come and embarrass you in front of the other diggers.

The showcase of urban archaeology is the work in York, which has led to the money-spinning reconstruction called the Jorvik Centre (Jorvik being the Viking word for York), where an endless queue of tourists is taken in electric cars round a mock-up of a Viking settlement built on the actual site. There are dummies in costume, sound-effects, and even appropriate smells (children especially like the latrine). If confronted by denigrators of this type of thing, bluffers should applaud its profits and its contribution to bringing the past to life vividly for the general public. If faced with a Jorvik admirer, however, you can wryly observe that it has done for archaeology what Mills & Boon have done for English literature.

Experimental Archaeology

One of the most entertaining branches of archaeology, this involves using ancient implements – or making and using replicas of them – to learn about their functions, capabilities, effectiveness, residues, etc. This gives you a chance to blow Tutankhamun's trumpets, steer an ox-drawn plough, fire arrows, throw spears, attack colleagues with bronze swords, burn down buildings and still call it scholarly research.

It can have its risky aspects: in the last century a certain Dr Robert Ball of Dublin tested some Irish horns of the Late Bronze Age, blew too hard, burst a blood vessel and died. Even today, makers of replica stone tools can be recognized by their chipped spectacles and the bandaids on their fingers.

Bluffers should refer disparagingly to:

a)   the unreliability, and
b)   the irrelevance
of the results of short-term experiments by unpractised hands. Archaeology covers such immense periods of time that it tends to be concerned with long-term trends – a century is a brief moment to archaeologists unless they are waiting for Directory Enquiries. Very few archaeological sites are 'frozen in time', giving an insight into short-term behaviour: Pompeii is one such site, where the end came so suddenly that people have been found doing all kinds of things they never meant posterity to see; and shipwrecks form another kind of 'time capsule'.

You can make the same objections to the equally short-term data acquired in:

Ethnoarchaeology

One of the latest branches of the subject, this is an excellent means of getting an exotic adventure holiday in a remote location. It involves picking on some unsuspecting group of people (hunter-gatherers, simple villagers, sheep farmers, etc.) – preferably in the Third World or Alaska. You then go and live among them for a while, taking note of how and when they make and use things, and how and when they break and discard them.

The victims are expected to tolerate nosy foreigners with notebooks and cameras camping on their doorstep and following them to the shops, workplace, kitchen, dining room and dustbin. Surprisingly, very few ethnoarchaeologists are violently attacked.

After figuring out what you think is going on with the use and discard of objects (you should never stay around long enough to master the language) you return to your desk and use these brief studies to make sweeping generalisations about what people in the past and in totally different environments must have done. This is part of what is called the:

New Archaeology – or rather, Archeology, since it has largely been perpetrated by Americans. Bluffers can take comfort from the fact that the title itself is a bluff. It is really Old Archaeology dressed up with jargon and presented with a fair degree of pomposity and bullying (see Theoretical Archaeology). The angry young men who started all the fuss in the 1960s indulged in a great deal of self-congratulation, mutual admiration and denigration (the viciousness of archaeological in-fighting is legendary), but when the dust settled it became clear that nothing much had changed and very little had been achieved.

When confronted by people who know something of New Archeology, you should respect its aspirations and its enterprise, but regret its wasted energy and ultimate lack of success. If faced with anyone else you can go to town, using obscure terms like 'Middle Range Theory' (don't worry about what it means, if anything; most archaeologists don't know either) or the 'Hypothetico-Deductive Method', or referring to the search for Universal Laws of Human Behaviour (the Holy Grail of New Archeology).

Be sure not to overdo it, or you will rapidly lose your audience. This kind of nonsense does not sound like real archaeology to them, or indeed to anyone other than New Archeologists.

Industrial Archaeology, and Garbage

Since archaeology is about all the traces of past human behaviour, it follows that everything thrown away – right up to this morning – can be counted as archaeological material. Thus a lot of very dedicated people devote their efforts to recording and preserving the relics of the recent industrial past (factories, machinery, mines, bridges, canals, etc.) to make sure that there is something left of it all for future archaeologists to study.

This means that broken fridges, discarded furniture, clapped out televisions and empty bottles can be argued to be archaeological artifacts. Even the material you consign to your dustbin – your own private little archaeological midden – may still attract the attention of some earnest seekers of data. In Arizona for some years they have been suffering the aptly named 'Garbage Project', whereby zealous archaeology students poke about in citizens' trash cans, classifying and quantifying what is thrown away.

This is supposed to give some insights into how and when people discard things (see Ethnoarchaeology), but, as any bluffer can point out, with only the faintest of smirks, how empty cans of dogmeat and used light bulbs can tell us much about any period in the past is not readily apparent to folk outside Arizona.

Museum Work

Finally, many archaeologists are based in museums, where their work entails:
a) looking after collections of objects that nobody ever studies
b) putting on exhibitions, and
c) thinking up ways to amuse and instruct the appalling hordes of screaming schoolchildren inflicted on them by desperate teachers.

Their lives are also blighted by occasional lunatics, and by an endless stream of citizens demanding to have some object identified which they have dug up in the garden or found on the beach. Not unnaturally a great many archaeologists encountered in the field are museum people who have managed a fleeting escape.

FAMOUS ARCHAEOLOGISTS

As very few archaeologists have ever become world famous, you will only need to know the basics about a select shortlist.

If stuck, simply make up some names, the more implausible the better: in recent years there have been archaeologists called Glob, Plog, Prat, Clot and Frankenstein. And there are so many archaeologists in the world that nobody can have heard of them all. When in a tight corner, you can escape in a single bound by citing recent work by some 'eminent' fictitious name from an obscure part of the world such as Paraguay, Albania or the University of Bradford. Do not, however, try a common name: there are umpteen eminent Clark(e)s and Smiths in archaeology, and you may be asked to specify which one you mean.

Nabonidus
The first known archaeologist was Nabonidus, the last king of Babylon. In the 6th century B.C. he and his daughter Princess En-nigaldi-Nanna dug (or rather got their minions to dig) beneath buildings and located the foundations of more ancient structures. As archaeology as such did not then exist the average Babylonian must have thought them completely potty – but then royalty can get away with anything.

Heinrich Schliemann (1822-1890)
Schliemann is the only 19th century archaeologist that most people have ever heard of, and he wasn't a professional archaeologist but a businessman. When he was eight, his father, a poor German pastor, gave him a book for Christmas which contained a picture of Troy

in flames. Heinrich became obsessed with this image, and vowed that he would find Homer's Troy one day (this underlines the dangers of exposing impressionable young minds to images of violence).

Having amassed one fortune in Russia and another in America, he retired at the age of 46 – a neat trick if you can manage it – to Anatolia (the competent bluffer will never say Turkey), looked around for a likely mound in a setting that fitted Homer's description, dug into it, and uncovered an ancient ruined town. He kept on digging and found a whole series of ancient towns, one on top of the next, until he reached the one he believed was Homer's. This feat gave rise to the adage 'if at first you don't succeed, Troy, Troy again.'

He also claimed to have discovered a hoard of gold objects in the site, and is said to have smuggled it through the Turkish customs by hiding it under the voluminous skirts of his beautiful Greek wife. It is unlikely that this would be a safe hiding place today.

Opinions are divided about whether Schliemann should be considered a pioneer of archaeology or simply a crude treasure-hunter, especially as he dug right through the layer he was looking for. Be sure to adopt the opposite view to your opponent's.

Boucher de Perthes (1788-1868)
A minor customs official, this Frenchman pioneered the collection and identification of early stone tools, and believed they were made by humans in a remote age. Most of his contemporaries thought he was a crank, and he stated that 'I observe a smile on the face of those to whom I speak.' This is still an occupational hazard in archaeology.

Boucher de Perthes made the fundamental error, copied by many excavators since, of paying his workers by the find. With a touching innocence he offered a large reward to the workman who first unearthed human remains in his sites. Not surprisingly the prize was claimed very quickly, and even less surprisingly the jawbone proved to be a fake.

General Pitt-Rivers (1827-1900)
The well-informed bluffer should know that this early pioneer's real name was Augustus Lane Fox. While a professional soldier, he came into a big inheritance, including large chunks of Dorset, on condition that he changed his name to Pitt-Rivers. He readily agreed to these terms, as the new name was no sillier than the old. A great eccentric, he compelled his tenants to attend brass band concerts in his park on Sunday afternoons, and tried to acclimatise yaks and llamas to an English habitat.

His digs were run with precision and discipline, like military exercises. This tradition was continued later by Mortimer Wheeler, another military man; a number of modern excavators still try to run their digs like little corporals.

Howard Carter (1874-1939)
Carter is famous because he found the tomb of Tutankhamun. After shifting 200,000 tons of sand and rock and finding nothing in six seasons of work, he deserved a little luck. The bluffer will counter talk of the treasures, or reminiscences of the London exhibition, with a disparaging attitude, referring to the vulgarity of an obsession with gold, and the unhealthy emphasis on glamour rather than information about the lives of ordinary ancient Egyptians. The really accomplished will claim to prefer the simpler aesthetic appeal of the later (and comparatively unknown gold funerary mask of the pharoah Psusennes to that of King Tut.

Henri Breuil (1877-1961)

A French priest, Breuil came to dominate the whole field of prehistory for decades, especially the subject of Ice Age cave art. During his long life he reckoned he'd spent about 700 days inside the caves, copying the art – so it is little wonder that he developed eye troubles. Breuil became so eminent that he was known as the 'Pope of prehistory', and many archaeologists, including Breuil himself unfortunately, came to believe he was infallible. One lifelong friend dared to disagree with him and was never spoken to again.

Sir Mortimer Wheeler (1890-1976)

An exemplary digger who tackled big sites, 'Rik' preferred those with a military slant, like the great British hillfort of Maiden Castle with its enormous defences and its war cemetery. He is best known to the public as a television personality, star panelist of the BBC's *Animal, Vegetable, Mineral?* in the 1950s. The fact that this quiz show featuring three archaeologists identifying objects was a huge success underlines how far television entertainment has progressed in the last 30 years.

The bluffer should know that Wheeler's wit, charisma, moustache, curved pipe, and roguish charm not only appealed to the viewers: he was an inveterate womaniser far into old age. He was also a consummate bluffer, winning odd questions on *A.V.M.* by previously swotting up the catalogue of the chosen museum or checking which objects had been removed from display.

Glyn Daniel (1914-1986)

The foremost historian of archaeology, and an expert on megalithic monuments, Daniel was better known to the public as a populariser of the subject, and as the gastronome who wrote *The Hungry Archaeologist in*

France. The personification of avuncular TV chairmen (complete with glasses and spotty bow tie) he was a leading exponent of the 'Archaeology as Fun' approach, easily the sanest attitude to the subject.

The Leakeys
There are few dynasties of archaeologists, and this one has become the principal soap opera in the field. Louis Leakey (1903-1972), the gruff, tough founder of the 'firm' struck it rich in East Africa's Rift Valley, where ancient tools and bones were to be found in great quantities. Since his death the family's head has been his widow, Mary, who continued their pioneering work at Olduvai Gorge and other sites. The couple, known affectionately as 'Bones and Stones' because of their respective specialities, had three sons, one of whom, 'R.E.', followed in his father's footsteps and continued to make important finds at regular intervals, including the skull named 1470 (some 2.8 million years old) despite persistent and fruitless attempts by rivals to overtake him with fossils that had cuter names like 'Lucy and 'The First Family'.

Probably the best known archaeologist in the world today is **Indiana Jones**. Although most professionals openly scoff at his adventures, and criticise the films for perpetuating the myth of the archaeologist as a romantic treasure-hunter on the trail of buried gold and lost civilisations, this is all bluff. Secretly they welcome any portion of the Jones mystique that rubs off on them, knowing that the very word 'archaeologist' now conjures up images of 'Indie', with a stunning lady in tow. In departments of archaeology at American universities it is not unusual to find, hanging on the back of office-doors, a bullwhip and a battered hat.

GLOSSARY

Activity area – Scatter of artifacts where archaeologists like to imagine that something happened.

Artifact – Any object that looks as if people made or used it.

B.P. – Nothing to do with petrol, simply an abbreviation for 'Before the Present'. As archaeologists tend to live in the past, their 'Present' is actually 1950.

Barrow – A tumulus.

Bipedalism – Good bluffing jargon for walking upright on two legs.

Culture – Archaeological term for regional groups of similar artifacts, often equated with different peoples. Also that which grows on mugs and plates in the excavation hut.

Dating methods – Courtship rituals adopted by archaeologists who want to share digs.

Early/Late – The first/second part of a period. A popular alternative system is Lower/Middle/Upper. Archaeologists love to divide periods, phases and cultures into handy chunks like this, with the lines drawn through gaps in the evidence.

Hypocaust – A floor under which hot air circulates and heats the room above. The meeting place of any symposium of archaeologists constitutes the perfect example.

Hypothesis – A guess.

Lecturer – One who talks in someone else's sleep.

Lifeway – Awful American term meaning 'way of life', as in 'prehistoric lifeways', but tolerable in comparison with the unspeakable 'prehistoric foodways'.

Living floor – Floor on which archaeologists think people lived.

Mastaba – Flat-topped type of Egyptian tomb for high-ranking officials and priests, its unfortunate name is the butt of many jokes but ensures that students remember it.

Megalith – A big stone.

Microlith – A little stone.

Midden – An accumulated heap of trash (UK); a glove without fingers (US).

Mummification – Method of preserving a dead body to maintain a lifelike appearance by removing the guts and drawing the brain out through the nose.

Neanderthal – Early human type that derives its name from bones found in the 19th century in the Neander Tal (valley) in West Germany. Bluffers can reveal that the valley itself was named after a German hymn-writer called Neumann who gave his name the Greek form of Neander (new man).

Necropolis – An area of tombs; a kind of city set apart for the dead, something like Cheltenham.

Palaeolithic – The first and longest period of prehistory, named after the Greek for 'old stone' (Palaeolithic). It is followed by the **Neolithic** (new stone) age, and in between inevitably, is the **Mesolithic** (middle stone) age. Each of them is futher subdivided into phases (see Early) and cultures, mostly named after sites.

Posthole – Any hole too small to be a storage pit.

Ritual – All-purpose explanation used where nothing else comes to mind.

Rock art – Nothing to do with album covers, but anything drawn, painted, carved or engraved on rock.

Secretary – One whose salary is in inverse proportion to her worth.

Spoilheap – Mound of discarded dirt resulting from an excavation, probably so called because it spoils the view.

Storage pit – Any hole too big to be a posthole

Stratigraphy – The different layers encountered in a site, one above the other. In general, given a pair of layers, the upper one is younger than the one that lies beneath.

Theoretical archaeology – Last resort of the desperate and illiterate.

Theory – A series of hypotheses.

Tumulus – A barrow.

Typology – The arrangement of tools, pottery, etc., into different categories according to shape, size, date, or function. It takes an unbearably tidy and organised mind to enjoy this kind of thing: Pitt-Rivers was a master of classification and German archaeologists revel in it.

THE BLUFFER'S GUIDES

Available at £1.95 and (new editions) £1.99 each

Accountancy
Advertising
Antiques
Archaeology
Ballet
Bird Watching
Bluffing
British Class
The Classics
Computers
Consultancy
Cricket
EEC
Espionage
Feminism
Finance
Fortune Telling
Golf
The Green Bluffer's Guide
Hi-Fi
Hollywood
Japan
Jazz
Journalism
Literature
Management

Marketing
Maths
Modern Art
Motoring
Music
The Occult
Opera
Paris
Philosophy
Photography
Poetry
PR
Public Speaking
Publishing
Racing
Seduction
Sex
Teaching
Television
Theatre
Top Secretaries
University
Weather Forecasting
Whisky
Wine
World Affairs

All these books are available at your local bookshop or newsagent, or can be ordered direct from the publisher. Just tick the titles you require. Prices and availability subject to change without notice.

Ravette Books Limited, 3 Glenside Estate, Star Road, Partridge Green, Horsham, West Sussex RH13 8RA.

Please send a cheque or postal order, and allow the following for postage and packing: UK 25p for one book and 10p for each additional book ordered.